MY BREAKFAST WITH JESUS

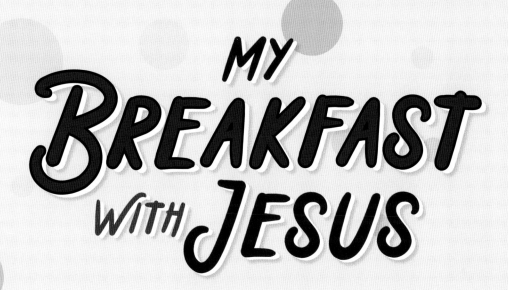

WRITTEN BY

Tina Cho

ILLUSTRATED BY

Guy Wolek

HARVEST KIDS

HARVEST HOUSE PUBLISHERS
EUGENE, OREGON

To my awesome agent, Adria, for this book idea—
may we share many more meals together.

The quote of Deuteronomy 12:7 is taken from The ESV® Bible (The Holy Bible, English Standard Version®), copyright © 2001 by Crossway, a publishing ministry of Good News Publishers. Used by permission. All rights reserved.

Cover design by Leah Beachy ＊ Interior design by Left Coast Design

My Breakfast with Jesus

Copyright © 2020 by Tina Cho
Artwork © 2020 by Guy Wolek
Published by Harvest House Publishers
Eugene, Oregon 97408
www.harvesthousepublishers.com

ISBN 978-0-7369-7712-8 (hardcover)

Library of Congress Cataloging-in-Publication Data Record
is available at https://lccn.loc.gov/2019035451

Printed in China

20 21 22 23 24 25 26 27 28 / LP / 10 9 8 7 6 5 4 3 2 1

There you shall eat before the Lord your God, and you shall rejoice, you and your households, in all that you undertake, in which the Lord your God has blessed you.

DEUTERONOMY 12:7

Many years ago, on a beach in Israel,
Jesus cooked breakfast for his friends.

Tired disciples ate delicious fish
prepared by the Fisher of men.

A **holy** way to start the day.
A breakfast blessing.

This lovely story comes from
the Bible in John 21.

These days, all around the world, family
and friends share Jesus's love at breakfast.

On a farm in Iowa, scents of
bacon, eggs, and cinnamon rolls
waft under bedroom doors.

Anna and Isaac spread icing
on gooey buns.

Mommy gets sticky hugs
as she reads a devotion.

A **hearty** way to start the day.
A breakfast blessing.

A locally sourced breakfast
wouldn't be complete without bacon
and eggs in this pork-producing state.
A cinnamon roll is a popular American
breakfast bread. The dough is rolled
in brown sugar and butter, baked,
and topped with icing.

Coffee diluted with milk warms
Mariana's mug in Brazil.

Her friends stop by so they can
walk to school together.

They gulp down ham and cheese
with bread and pray together over school.

A **peppy** way to start the day.
A breakfast blessing.

Some Brazilian children drink coffee,
which parents believe helps them
stay alert throughout the day.
Brazil is the largest producer
of coffee in the world.

Chocolate sprinkles decorate
buttered bread in the Netherlands.

Devon prepares a gift for his
parents—breakfast in bed.

They hold hands and
give thanks to God.

A **sweet** way to start the day.
A breakfast blessing.

Hagelslag is a favorite
morning treat. Chocolate is
sprinkled on buttered bread.
Sprinkles come in fruity flavors too.

On a street in Ghana,
Afi smells fried koose.

Her friend doesn't have enough
money to give the vendor.

Afi buys hausa koko
and koose for two.

A **loving** way
to start the day.
A breakfast blessing.

Hausa koko is millet porridge mixed
with chili peppers and other seasonings.
Koose is black-eyed peas, onions, and
chili peppers mixed with water
and eggs and deep fat fried.

Vermicelli sizzles, and the smell of saffron drifts to Kareema's room in the United Arab Emirates.

"Thank you, Mother, for making balaleet for our family."

Together they read Psalm 23
and pray for the day.

A **flavorful** way to start the
day. A breakfast blessing.

Balaleet is a sweet Emirate dish
of vermicelli noodles, eggs,
cardamom, and saffron.

In a village in India, lentils cook.
Priya tops her idlis with ghee.

Down the road, she shares food with a family, just as Jesus did with his friends.

A **caring** way to start the day.
A breakfast blessing.

Idlis are steamed, fermented black lentils and rice cakes topped with chutney, a spicy sauce with fruits and herbs, or ghee, a liquid butter.

Syrniki fry until they are golden brown in Russia.

Dmitri rolls dough with Babushka and sings hymns.

A friend who doesn't
get breakfasts will
be fed today.

A **musical** way
to start the day.
A breakfast blessing.

Syrniki are made of cottage cheese,
egg, flour, salt, and sugar. They are fried
and topped with sour cream or jam.

Beef noodle soup bubbles,
and baozi steams.

Soft, secret praises rise from an
underground church in China.

Noodles are a sign of long life in China.
Baozi are Chinese dumplings.

Lin Wong loves learning
about Jesus in the safe house.

A **quiet** way to start the day.
A breakfast blessing.

Halmoni rises before the sun
to attend morning prayer in Korea.

She prepares food for loved ones and finds
that a grandchild has made green tea.

Soybean paste soup, kimchi, rice, seaweed,
and a fried egg wait on a low table.

A **spicy** way to start the day.
A breakfast blessing.

Kimchi is fermented cabbage. Roasted
and salted seaweed is wrapped around
rice. Soybean paste soup has anchovies,
potatoes, zucchini, and onions. Green
tea is grown throughout Korea.
Halmoni means "grandmother."

Talking to people like Jesus did, Oliver
and a new friend exchange breakfasts—
smashed avocado toast and a cereal bar
for a beautiful blue emu egg.

Sunbeams lighten golden earth as this family
worships in the Australian outback.

A **breathtaking** way to start the day.
A breakfast blessing.

A common Australian breakfast is biscuit
cereal of wheat fiber that can be soaked
in milk. Smashed avocados provide
a creamy spread for toast. Aborigine
breakfasts can consist of emu eggs
and bread with nectar or honey.

At the bottom of the world in
Antarctica at the Chapel of the Snow,
a scientist and chaplain share fresh baked
bread and marvel at God's creation.

Penguins waddle. Seals bask. Glaciers glide.

A **frosty** way to start the day.
A breakfast blessing.

From 250 to 1000 scientists do research in Antarctica. Food and supplies are flown or shipped to the bases. Chefs prepare typical meals, and vegetables are grown in special greenhouses.

Beneath the stars in blackest space,
an astronaut prays over countries below.

Pouches of juice, bread, scrambled eggs,
and coffee float through the space station.

God, you are an amazing Creator.

A **heavenly** way to start the day.
A breakfast blessing.

Astronauts aboard the International Space Station eat breakfasts from dehydrated or dried food packets. They can add water to them or heat them.

For more than 2,000 years,
people around the world have started
their day with food in their bellies,
prayers on their tongues,
and Jesus in their hearts.

A breakfast blessing.

About the Author

Tina Cho is a teacher and the author of
Rice from Heaven and *Korean Celebrations*.
She has also written more than 100 guided reading
books for various educational publishers. Tina
grew up in Iowa but is currently living
and teaching in South Korea.

About the Artist

Guy Wolek has worked as a freelance artist
for more than 35 years on a wide range of projects,
including courtroom sketches, character development,
art direction, and illustration. His client list
includes several major US corporations
and publishing companies.